GIRL VS DIVORCE

Ken Harrip LL.B.

About the Author

Ken Harrip is a former lawyer who graduated with a Bachelor of Laws degree from the Queensland University of Technology and was admitted to the legal profession in 1994 as a Solicitor of the Supreme Court of Queensland. He practised predominantly in family law matters for a number of years and is a member of the Family Law Section of the Law Council of Australia. He has extensive experience of advising clients across a broad range of family law issues, such as separation; divorce; the division of marital assets (including family businesses with complex financial structures); spousal maintenance; shared parenting; child support; alternative dispute resolution processes; and domestic violence. Ken is a former overall winner of the Windsurfer Class Championships for the state of Queensland, Australia, and has twice been selected to represent Australia at a world windsurfing championship (the first time as a reserve). His other interests include aviation, music and cosmology.

Published by Ken Harrip 2021

Copyright © Ken Harrip 2021

The author asserts his moral rights in this work.

All rights reserved. No part of this book may be reproduced or transmitted by any person or entity, including internet search engines and retailers, in any form or by any means, electronic or mechanical, including photocopying and recording, or by any information storage and retrieval system, without the prior written permission of the publisher.

A catalogue record for this book is available from the National Library of Australia

ISBN 978-0-6451883-0-1 (paperback)
ISBN 978-0-6451883-1-8 (ebook)

Cover design © The Brewster Project
Text design by Mary Callahan Design

Disclaimer

This book is intended to be a source of valuable information for the reader, but it is of the nature of general comment only and is not provided as legal, financial, psychological or other advice. No lawyer-client, financial adviser-client or registered clinical psychologist-client relationship is formed. This book has been written without knowledge or consideration of the reader's individual circumstances or needs and should not be relied on as the basis for any reader's decision to act, or refrain from acting, on any matter which it covers. No reader should rely on the contents of this book without first obtaining advice from a lawyer, a professional financial adviser, a registered clinical psychologist or other professional person, as appropriate. This book is sold on the terms and understanding that neither the author, the editor, nor any person who has approved any part of the content of this book or who has contributed to the content of this book is responsible for the results of any actions taken or not taken on the basis of information in this book. To the fullest extent permitted by law the author, the editor, and any person who has approved any part of the content of this book or who has contributed to the content of this book expressly disclaims all and any liability and responsibility to any person, whether a purchaser or reader of this book or not, in respect of anything, and of the consequences of anything, done or omitted to be done by any such person in reliance, whether wholly or partially, upon the whole or any part of the contents of this book. Your use of this book implies your acceptance of this disclaimer.

For Fiona, with love

CONTENTS

Acknowledgments ix
Introduction 1
1 The First Rule of Divorce 11
2 Smart Decisions, A Happier Life 29
3 Money, Money, Money 37
4 Proven Ways to Avoid Arguments 49
5 Your Children Come First:
   Making a Success of Shared Parenting 55
6 Make Self-Care a Priority 65
7 Alone But Not Lonely 71
8 Domestic Violence – How to Protect
   Yourself and Your Family 77
9 Same-Sex Divorce – The Special Challenges 89
10 Looking for Love Again 99

ACKNOWLEDGMENTS

At the outset I express my profound gratitude to my editor, who prefers to be anonymous. Her overarching contribution to this book was substantial. She gave generously of her time, her editorial expertise, her professional guidance and her personal support. Her involvement in this project was invaluable to me. Thank you very much, Ed.

I am most grateful to clinical psychologist Sophie Jordan for reviewing Chapter 5 and for confirming that the content of that chapter conforms to 'best practice' as understood by psychologists who work in the area of shared parenting after separation or divorce. I am also indebted to her for suggesting a number of valuable additions to the chapter, stressing the importance of both parents being fully aware of two crucial principles of shared parenting after separation or divorce. First, parents jointly share duties and responsibilities concerning the care, welfare and development of their children. Second, provided that it isn't contrary to their best interests to do so, such as when they would be at risk of physical or psychological harm, children have a right to spend time on a regular basis with, and communicate on a regular basis with, both of their parents as well as with other people significant to their care, welfare and development, such as grandparents and other relatives.

In addition to her clinical practice, Sophie provides a range of services to the legal sector, including the preparation of so-called Family Reports. These reports take the form of an independent assessment of the issues in disputed shared parenting cases and can help a judge hearing a case to make decisions about arrangements for the children. In that capacity she is regularly called as a witness to give evidence in court. Sophie is a registered Family Dispute Resolution Practitioner and often acts as an independent child-inclusive expert in child-centred mediation.

I owe a special thank-you to Fiona, who spent countless hours brainstorming ideas for this book and sharing her razor-sharp insight with me. Thank you so much, Mate.

I am forever indebted to lawyers John Hutchinson and Gary Hutchinson, the then partners of Cooke and Hutchinson Solicitors, Brisbane, Australia, where I served my articles of clerkship and was subsequently employed as a lawyer and later as an associate of the firm. During my articles of clerkship, John (as my master) and Gary provided me with a first-class training environment in which to learn the skills and values necessary to practise as a lawyer. In every aspect of legal practice they led by example and gave extensively of their time to share with me their legal knowledge and experience. I have the deepest respect for John and Gary on a professional and personal level. (They each have a great sense of humour, too, which is extremely helpful given the demands of legal practice!) We remain good friends. I offer them my sincere gratitude.

A big thank-you to my family for their love and support. I am deeply grateful to my mother for being her loving and generous self and for all that she has done for me over the years. A retired English teacher, she was always very enthusiastic about the idea of this book and has taken great delight in following the process of writing and editing. Her excitement in the lead-up to the book's release was palpable. Thanks, Bud.

I wish to acknowledge the depth of support I receive on an ongoing basis from my inner circle of friends and my trusted professional advisers of many years. Their kindness, wit and counsel have added, and continue to add, immeasurably to the quality of my life. Thank you, everyone.

Finally, I wholeheartedly thank the women who candidly shared with me their own stories of separation and divorce after I left legal practice and began writing this book. They inspired me to continue writing.

For information on the special challenges inherent in same-sex divorce, I am indebted to Abbie E. Goldberg and Adam P. Romero (ed.), *LGBTQ Divorce and Relationship Dissolution: Psychological and Legal Perspectives and Implications for Practice*, Oxford University Press, New York, 2019.

The poem 'Love Comes Quietly' by Robert Creeley, the opening line of which is quoted in Chapter 10, appears in the volume *For Love: Poems*, copyright © 1962 by Robert Creeley.

A note to the reader
Girl vs Divorce has been specifically designed to meet the needs of readers not just in Australia but across a range of comparable countries and jurisdictions, including the United Kingdom, the United States and Canada. While some specifics may vary from country to country, there is a great deal of common ground when it comes to the challenges, both legal and non-legal, that divorce typically presents.

INTRODUCTION

The process of separation and divorce is widely considered to be the second most stressful life event, surpassed only by the death of a loved one. With the end of a marriage there most often comes a prolonged period of emotional turbulence, accompanied by far-reaching practical challenges and lifestyle changes. Almost every area of life may be thrown into disarray. Depending on the individual circumstances, it's common for women and men alike to experience intense feelings of grief and loneliness, and these may be compounded by anxiety if the divorce settlement has left either or both in a substantially weaker financial position – or, worse, in dire financial straits. (The whole area of divorce and its aftermath has been well researched over the years by various government departments and other stakeholders. A wide range of interesting studies and reports is readily available online.)

While I fully acknowledge the heavy toll that divorce and its aftermath take on both parties (and their children, if any), as a lawyer who practised predominantly in family law matters for a number of years I came to identify a need for a book like this, written specifically for women who are embarking on, or in the process of recovering from, a separation or divorce – but also for those who continue to face challenges and difficulties arising out of their divorce long into the future – for two main reasons.

First and foremost, I know from my own experience as a practising lawyer that after the breakdown of a marriage not all women receive a just and equitable share of the marital assets. Nor, if applicable, are they all paid the levels of spousal maintenance and child support to which they are legally entitled. (Spousal maintenance is the term used in Australia and the United Kingdom, while in the United States spousal maintenance is commonly known as alimony, and in Canada it is referred to as spousal support.) In other words, some women receive an unjust divorce settlement. Generally speaking, this happens for one of two reasons:

1. Their legal rights are deliberately violated by their husband by means of duress, fraud, the concealment of marital assets, or some other kind of dishonest or illegal strategy. This can occur regardless of whether they are aware of their legal rights, and even to women who have full-time legal representation. (See Chapter 1 for more on this.)

2. Their legal rights are not deliberately violated by their husband but they fail to enforce their rights. This can happen for a number of reasons, but the following are among the most common.

    ▶ They agree to a divorce settlement proposed by their husband without first obtaining legal advice and are unaware that the terms of the settlement are unjust.

    ▶ The legal advice they obtain is incorrect. This most often occurs when their lawyer has little or no experience in family law matters. It may also occur when they retain the lawyer who is also representing their husband (a grave mistake, as explained in Chapter 1).

- ▶ They have been correctly advised as to their rights by a lawyer (or, not having been so advised, are nonetheless aware of their rights) but forgo those rights and knowingly agree to a settlement that is unjust. This decision is sometimes based on feelings of guilt – for example, if they initiated the separation – or simply on a desire to 'just get it over with', because they are so distressed by the divorce that they are unable to continue negotiations. (I have personally represented women who fall into the latter category. Unfortunately, in those cases my clients were so distraught by the separation that they chose not to take my advice that the settlement proposed by their husband was unjust and ought to be rejected. They agreed to settle on the husband's terms to bring the formalities to an end as quickly as possible and thereby alleviate the extreme distress occasioned by that process.)

The stories of the separated or divorced women I have spoken with since leaving legal practice and undertaking research for this book have confirmed that unjust divorce settlements and their consequences are ongoing problems.

There is a crucially important fact that women need to know about these kinds of divorce settlement injustices. In many cases they are entirely *preventable* – and, if such an injustice has already taken place, in limited cases it can be put right. (If you believe that you have fallen victim to an unjust divorce settlement, you should obtain legal advice as a matter of urgency. Overturning injustices of this kind may require an application to a court, and time limits may apply.)

It is, therefore, abundantly clear to me that women who are considering or going through a separation or a divorce need a resource like this book that clearly alerts them to the importance of obtaining legal advice prior to, or at the earliest opportunity after, separation – even if the separation is amicable – and that makes them fully aware of the potentially disastrous effect on their future of failing to enforce their legal rights.

Second, in the course of my work as a lawyer I was regularly witness to the acute stress and emotional suffering many women experience during the divorce process. But it was also apparent that some women's distress continued long into the future. This was particularly so in cases where the separation was acrimonious and it was necessary for the women to have ongoing contact with their ex-husband, usually because they shared the care of children.

Problems with parenting arrangements and disputes over the payment of child support – either or both of which often led to frequent arguments with their ex – made life a living hell for some women, forcing them to seek further legal advice, and sometimes to take legal action against their ex, long after their divorce had been finalised. This both delayed their recovery and significantly affected the quality of their life. Such cases acted as additional motivation for me to undertake further research into the experience of divorce as a whole and, specifically, into the practical ways by which at least some of this distress can be alleviated.

So, drawing on both my professional experience and my research, I feel confident in saying this: In addition to the many other variables that play a part in the process of recovery from divorce, there are two very reliable predictors of both the severity of the distress women are likely to suffer during the formal divorce process and what their future is likely to hold in terms of their standard of living and the quality of their post-divorce life.

The first predictor is whether or not they obtained a fair and just legal settlement. The importance of this cannot be over-stressed. While the prevalence of violations of women's legal rights and of unjust settlements, such as those mentioned above, is not fully understood and is therefore difficult to quantify, and every woman's circumstances are unique, this is an issue that blights the lives of too many women. Chapter 1 covers these and related issues in some detail.

Having said this, I wish to make it clear that I don't suggest for a moment that after separation most men set out to deprive their wife of a just and equitable legal outcome. On the contrary, many couples separate and divorce on a reasonably amicable basis without major disagreement on any legal or practical issues. Some maintain a friendship long after the divorce has been finalised. Nor do I in any way imply that men are never disadvantaged as the result of divorce settlements. There are many possible scenarios in this complex area, but they are not the subject of this book.

The second predictor is how well prepared and equipped a woman is for what lies ahead. Divorce is a life crisis like no other. It is a uniquely challenging experience for which few are adequately prepared. (This statement applies equally to men, of course, but for the reasons stated previously the focus of this book is on women.) Since most women go through a divorce only once in their life, they are likely to be unaware of the magnitude of the challenges they will face. Many will be confronted by difficulties that they have not had to deal with previously and couldn't have foreseen – and, as a consequence, some may not be practised in the particular skills they will need to help them to cope with these challenges and difficulties.

In writing this book I have set out to address these two key issues by providing women with clear, well-researched information that will help them to approach both the legal aspects of the divorce process and some of the most common post-divorce challenges they are likely to encounter with a considerable degree of confidence.

The core theme of this book is that while, for most people, divorce is a deeply disturbing life crisis, there are steps you can take that will go a long way towards alleviating at least some of the stress involved, both during the divorce process itself and in your life post-divorce. By adopting a 'divorce management' mindset and making use of the proven strategies set out in this book, you can stay in control of your circumstances and make the whole experience of divorce considerably less distressing than it might otherwise be – and, in so doing, ease your transition to this new stage of your life. You will then be in a much stronger position to cope with whatever challenges you may encounter further down the track. Remember: Unless you personally take control of your divorce, your divorce will almost certainly take control of you.

Girl vs Divorce consists of 10 chapters, each devoted to a specific aspect of the divorce experience taken as a whole. In the first eight chapters you will find proven strategies that will help you to:

- Obtain justice in the settlement of the legal aspects of your divorce.

- Make decisions that are likely to serve your best interests and those of your family, both now and in the long term.

- Take control of your finances by (if necessary) brushing up on the fundamental principles of good money management.

- Avoid arguments with your ex.

- Make a success of shared parenting.

- Take care of your physical and emotional well-being during one of the most stressful experiences of your life.

- Live on your own, if you choose or need to do so, without succumbing to loneliness.

- Protect yourself and your family from domestic violence (if you are among the far too many women who are victims of this scourge).

Chapter 9 deals with the unique challenges same-sex couples may face when going through a divorce. And finally, the book provides some practical and commonsense guidance on finding love again in a world where dating is most likely very different from what it was before you were married.

Girl vs Divorce applies equally to women going through or recovering from a divorce and to those going through or recovering from a separation from a partner with whom they were living in a legally recognised domestic relationship – and much of the information in this book may also be helpful to women in the same situation who were living in a domestic relationship that is not legally recognised.

Should anyone question the title *Girl vs Divorce*, I chose the term 'girl' for two simple reasons. First, because it makes for an appealing and memorable title. Second – a related point – because of its informal quality, analogous to the much-used male equivalent, 'guy'.

While I can't possibly (and don't, of course) promise anyone a happy future, it's my sincere hope that the information in this book will help to set women who are going through a separation or divorce on the right path towards achieving that goal. I wish you all courage and success.

Ken Harrip
September 2021

》》 *Above all, be the heroine of your life, not the victim.*

NORA EPHRON
AMERICAN JOURNALIST, WRITER AND FILMMAKER

CHAPTER 1

The First Rule of Divorce

>>> *I not only use all the brains I have, but all that I can borrow.*

WOODROW WILSON
FORMER PRESIDENT OF THE UNITED STATES

FIRST AND FOREMOST, your divorce is a legal matter, and it may well be the most important legal matter of your life. Your marriage must be formally dissolved by a court order. Marital assets and debts need to be divided justly according to law. Your husband may have a legal obligation to pay spousal maintenance (variously known as spousal support or alimony) to you. And arrangements may have to be made for the ongoing care and financial support of children.

Every woman has the indisputable right to a just and equitable settlement of these legal issues. Because there's so much at stake, most women who have successfully negotiated a divorce will tell you that obtaining justice in the legal aspects of their divorce is the crucial first step on the road to recovery. So it's essential that you obtain expert legal advice from the outset, assert your rights strenuously, and hold out for the legal settlement you're entitled to. This cannot be overstressed. This is the first rule of divorce.

Regrettably, some women don't do this. They then learn the hard way that the legal and financial consequences of divorce can be devastating. To put it bluntly, if you don't seek expert advice from a suitably qualified and experienced lawyer, and don't take the proper steps to enforce your legal rights, you could pay for this mistake for the rest of your life.

The benefits of engaging a lawyer

An experienced lawyer will look after your legal and financial interests and guide you through the divorce process as smoothly as possible. Without one, you risk stumbling through your life dogged by regrets.

Having an experienced lawyer on your side will also do a great deal to make you feel empowered at this difficult and stressful time. Your lawyer will:

- Devise the strategy that is most likely to result in the best legal outcome for you. This will involve anticipating any likely problems, including problems you are unlikely to be aware of. Your lawyer will take steps to prevent or resolve them.

- Negotiate on your behalf with your husband or his lawyer. This is particularly helpful if relations between you and your ex are strained or, worse, if he is behaving in an intimidating or abusive way. Your lawyer will deal with him so that you can avoid hostile confrontations.

- Engage any experts needed to support your case.

- Explain the alternative dispute resolution (ADR) processes available to help you reach an out-of-court settlement with your husband. One such process is mediation, in which an impartial and highly trained lawyer assists you both to identify the issues in dispute and find a productive way to negotiate a settlement.

- Prepare the necessary legal documents and appear on your behalf in court should negotiations fail to resolve the legal aspects of your divorce and you decide to initiate court proceedings against your ex or need to defend court proceedings initiated by him.

A further benefit of being represented by a lawyer is that lawyers who work exclusively or predominantly in certain areas of law, such as family law, are usually familiar with the idiosyncrasies of the various judges and know how they tend to interpret the laws governing cases like yours. This means that your lawyer may be able to advise you in advance whether the judge who is to hear your case is likely to find for or against you on a particular legal issue. Your lawyer may also know your husband's lawyer, either personally or by reputation. All these things will help your lawyer to present your case in the way most likely to achieve a favourable result for you.

A lawyer will uphold your right to justice

During the divorce process an appropriately qualified and experienced lawyer will advise you as to your legal rights and responsibilities, advance and defend your interests diligently, and do all they can to ensure the best possible legal outcome for you in your circumstances.

To this end your lawyer will:

- Ensure that you receive an equitable share of the marital assets. Remember that you may have worked very hard for a large part of your life to help accumulate those assets.

- Advise you as to whether you're entitled to spousal maintenance and, if so, ensure that the amount of spousal maintenance agreed upon by you and your ex (or the amount that has been calculated by a judge) is the correct amount under the applicable law. (After a divorce an ex-husband doesn't always have a responsibility to pay spousal maintenance to his ex-wife. This issue is dealt with on a case-by-case basis.)

- If applicable, advise you as to your children's rights and your responsibilities under the laws relating to shared parenting.

Your lawyer will also assist you to negotiate a shared parenting agreement that is not only in your children's best interests but also specifies the routines and schedules agreed upon in precise and unambiguous terms. This will significantly reduce the likelihood of future disagreements with your ex about the terms of your agreement.

- If applicable, a lawyer will also advise you as to whether either party is legally obliged to make child support payments to the other. This is potentially a complicated issue and is decided on a case-by-case basis.

In order to ensure that you obtain a just legal outcome, your lawyer will:

- Take steps, if necessary, to see that you don't fall victim to duress, fraud or any other dishonest or illegal strategy on your husband's part – such as the concealment of marital assets – that is intended to deprive you of your fair share of the marital assets or, if applicable, spousal maintenance or child support.

- Help you to avoid being ruled by your emotions at a time when you are most likely feeling distressed and vulnerable, and guide you to make rational and intelligent decisions that are right for you, not only now but in the long term. For example, if you were the one who initiated the separation and divorce, you may be overcome by feelings of guilt and be tempted to try to make amends by giving your ex a larger share of the marital assets than he is entitled to receive or by forgoing a right to spousal maintenance, if you have such a right. This might seem like a good idea at the time but may leave you at a serious financial disadvantage in the future. At the very least, your lawyer will make sure you fully understand the consequences of your actions.

Choosing the right kind of lawyer

Just as you wouldn't ask your local doctor to perform a hip replacement but would request a referral to a specialist orthopaedic surgeon, so too your best plan is to engage a lawyer who practises exclusively or predominantly in the area of family law. This is the kind of lawyer you want on your side: a family law expert. Don't settle for anything less.

So, how do you go about finding a family law expert? The following are all reliable ways of doing this.

- The jurisdiction in which your divorce is being dealt with will most likely have a peak professional body responsible for, among other things, promoting excellence in the legal profession in that jurisdiction. Just three examples are The Law Society of New South Wales in Australia; the Law Society of England and Wales; and The State Bar of California. Many such bodies maintain a publicly accessible register of lawyers who have completed a specialist training course in family law. In Australia and the United Kingdom such lawyers can then advertise themselves as accredited specialists in the field, while in the United States and Canada they are known as certified specialists.

    To become accredited (or certified) as a family law specialist, lawyers are usually required to have a proven level of experience in family law and to demonstrate a genuine interest in the field. They are also usually required to undertake ongoing study and professional development. This means that when you consult an accredited (or certified) family law specialist you can be confident that they know all the ins and outs of family law and are in a position to achieve the best outcome for you that your circumstances permit. You can find the law society or bar association in your area by typing 'law society or bar association near me' into an internet search engine.

- In addition to accredited (or certified) family law specialists, there are many lawyers who have outstanding skill, knowledge and experience in the area of family law and are highly regarded as experts in the field. Try typing 'family law experts near me' into an internet search engine. This should produce a list of law firms in your area that advertise that they practise in the area of family law. Click the link to the website of three or four of the listed firms. Many such websites provide details of the level of experience and the specific areas of expertise of each lawyer in the firm. This will help you to determine if the firm might be a good fit for you.

- Try telephoning a large law firm that does not handle divorce cases. Again, you'll be able to find one by searching the internet. Ask to speak to a lawyer in the litigation section of the firm and explain that you are seeking a recommendation for a lawyer to represent you in your divorce proceedings. They may be able to recommend someone to you on the spot. If not, a good lawyer will most likely offer to make enquiries on your behalf and phone you back with a list of names.

- Government-funded legal authorities (such as Legal Aid), community legal centres and women's legal services (all of which you can find on the internet) may similarly provide you with a list of names of family law experts in your area. Organisations such as these may also provide you with a one-off legal advice consultation with a family law expert (or, in limited circumstances, full-time legal representation) for free. More on this later.

- Other professionals (especially someone you know and trust) who work in the area of family law, such as accountants, psychologists and social workers, may be able to recommend such a lawyer to you.

Engaging your ex's lawyer – a critical error

Under no circumstances should you engage the lawyer who is representing your husband in the divorce. Surprisingly, this is not unheard of, despite the fact that lawyers have an ethical obligation to avoid acting concurrently for two parties who have adverse interests in a legal dispute. What is more important for you, it could also result in your receiving a much less favourable legal settlement than you would have received had you been represented by an independent lawyer.

Try before you buy

Chemistry is critical to your relationship with your lawyer, so before you make your choice make a list of at least three lawyers who specialise in family law and then phone their offices. Assuming they can accommodate you in their upcoming schedule, ask if you can arrange a brief meeting (of about 20 minutes), at no cost to you, to assess whether you are compatible and likely to be able to work together successfully. This is common practice, so there is no need to feel awkward about doing this. A good lawyer will respect you for showing such good sense.

How to develop a productive relationship with your lawyer

There are a number of things you can do to help you and your lawyer work together more effectively. Here are some suggestions:

- ▶ Be open and honest. Especially during your first consultation, you may feel a bit embarrassed about discussing your private life with your lawyer, including personal matters you may have kept entirely to yourself until now. This is only natural, but there is no need to be embarrassed. The first thing to remember is that family lawyers are professionals who deal with such matters day in and day out. There is little, if indeed anything, you can say that your lawyer won't have heard before. The second thing to remember is that your lawyer needs to know everything that is relevant to your situation in order to achieve the best possible resolution of all the disputed legal issues. If you are less than completely open and honest, you are the one who will suffer the consequences, possibly for the rest of your life.

- During your first meeting tell your lawyer what's most important to you and the legal result you want to achieve. You should also inform your lawyer of any immediate concerns you may have. For example, you may have a well-founded fear that your husband has sold (or is intending to sell) a valuable marital asset without your consent and has concealed (or intends to conceal) the proceeds of sale so that they cannot be traced and shared with you.

- Ask your lawyer to confirm all your instructions in writing. This helps to prevent any misunderstandings.

- Think carefully about the postal address, email address and telephone numbers you give to your lawyer, and don't give your lawyer any postal or email address that your ex might have access to.

- Let your lawyer know that you want to be actively involved in your case as far as possible. If you have any suggestions or think you know of a better way of approaching a particular issue, speak up! If your idea won't work, your lawyer will tell you so.

- Tell your lawyer immediately about any significant and relevant events that occur during the divorce process, such as your ex contacting you privately and exerting pressure on you to agree to a settlement that is likely to result in an unjust legal result for you. It's important to resolve any such problems quickly, so your lawyer needs to know about them as soon as they occur.

- Your lawyer will build your case on information, much of it in the form of paperwork. You will be given or sent a list of the documents required. Some of these documents may seem unimportant to you, but you need to trust your lawyer's judgment. The foundation of a strong legal case is irrefutable evidence, and these documents will form part or all of the evidence needed to strengthen your legal case. Gathering this documentary evidence will require some effort on your part, but by doing so you give yourself leverage and power. So, if you want to optimise your prospects of obtaining justice in your divorce settlement, it is critically important that you provide your lawyer with the required documents as soon as you can.

- Your lawyer will have to navigate through a lot of information, so make this job easier by organising your documents as best you can. If a document is comprised of multiple pages (such as a bank statement), staple the pages together and use a highlighter pen to draw your lawyer's attention to any parts of the document that may be of particular importance to your case.

- Before every consultation, write all your questions down. This will save time and, ultimately, money. It will also help to ensure that during the consultation you don't completely forget that critically important question you wanted to ask. Never be afraid to tell your lawyer if there is anything you don't understand about any stage of the process. The law can be complicated and confusing, even for lawyers. In divorce cases, there is no such thing as a silly question.

- Take notes during phone calls, consultations and court appearances. You cannot expect to recall everything that was discussed on each occasion, let alone recall it reasonably accurately, if you don't do this.

- Your lawyer will need to correspond with your husband or his lawyer on a regular basis. They may also need to prepare many legal documents on your behalf. Some of the correspondence or legal documents will be sent to you in draft form for your approval. Read all drafts carefully to ensure that they are accurate and that they correctly reflect your instructions. If the draft correspondence or documents consist of more than one page, check the page numbering to ensure that you've received all the pages; sometimes pages can be missed as a result of photocopying errors.

- Treat all correspondence from your lawyer as urgent. Read it and respond without delay, as delay can be harmful to your case.

- Family lawyers will nearly always be handling several cases at any one time and have a busy schedule of client conferences, court appearances and so on. Clearly, you cannot expect your lawyer to be available to speak to you whenever you call, but you can expect that your lawyer or someone from your lawyer's office will respond to your calls promptly.

- Similarly, if your lawyer leaves a message asking you to call back, you should do so as soon as possible.

- Accept that there may be periods of inactivity. This is to be expected in the course of legal proceedings.

- Remember that your lawyer is an expert in family law; that and that alone is what you are paying for. Your lawyer is not a mental health professional or a social worker. The majority of people who choose to practise in the area of family law are reasonably sensitive and sympathetic by nature, but that is as far as it goes. If your lawyer interrupts you when you want to talk about psychological or emotional issues, this is not out of rudeness or insensitivity. By keeping you on track your lawyer is acting in your best interests and saving you money. If you need a mental health professional, your lawyer may be able to refer you to one.

- ▶ Keep abreast of developments in your case. Ask your lawyer to update you regularly (but within reason).
- ▶ Don't let the tail wag the dog. It's your life and your divorce, and you alone must make the decisions that feel right to you. Your lawyer can and will advise you of the legal consequences of your decisions, but a good lawyer will not try to push you into doing something you don't want to do.
- ▶ Keep firmly in mind that your lawyer cannot guarantee what the outcome of your case will be. The outcome depends on the facts presented by both sides, the law, and – if you have to go to court – the judge's view of your case. No two divorce cases are exactly alike. Your lawyer may or may not express an opinion as to the likelihood of a particular outcome, but no one knows in advance what the outcome will be.

'But I can't afford full-time legal representation'

Believe me, if you want to give yourself the best chance of receiving a just and equitable divorce settlement, you can't afford not to retain a lawyer to represent you. Lawyers don't come cheap, that's true. But good lawyers can be worth their weight in gold. If, however, your financial situation is a bit precarious right now and there is no room in your budget to pay for ongoing legal services, don't despair – you still have several good options:

- ▶ Many lawyers are willing to dispense with monthly invoices and take their entire fee in a lump sum at the conclusion of your case when you receive your share of the marital assets. This kind of arrangement is common in divorce cases.

- You may be able to find a law firm that is willing to advise or represent you on a pro bono basis. (Pro bono means 'free' or 'without charge'.) Try searching 'pro bono lawyers near me' on the internet.
- You may be eligible for government-funded legal representation (sometimes called Legal Aid).
- Not-for-profit women's legal services or the like may provide you with full-time legal representation. You'll find services like these by searching the internet for 'free legal advice near me' or 'free legal advice for women near me'.

Going it alone

For a range of reasons too diverse and complicated to cover here, some women will be unable to find a lawyer who will provide full-time representation for them. If this applies to you – or if for some other reason you prefer to deal with the legal aspects of your divorce on your own – and you want to be fully and correctly informed about your legal rights before you begin negotiating directly with your ex or his lawyer, here's what to do in seven steps:

1. Set aside, or borrow if necessary, enough money to pay for a single consultation (of about one to two hours) with a family law expert of your choice at a law firm. If you can't afford to do this, try phoning all the law firms in your area that offer pro bono legal services and ask for a one-off appointment with one of their family law experts. If neither of these strategies is successful, contact your nearest women's legal service, community legal centre or Legal Aid office and ask for a one-off appointment with a family law expert.

2. When you make your appointment, ask what documents you should bring with you. If the person you speak to is unable to answer your question, ask if a list

of the documents can be emailed or mailed to you. Alternatively, go to the website of a law firm that specialises in family law. That website will most likely set out details of the documents that new clients should bring to their first interview.

3. At your appointment, explain that you're going through a divorce and can't afford or otherwise don't qualify for full-time legal representation – or, as the case may be, that you wish to deal with the legal side of your divorce on your own – and will be conducting all negotiations with your ex or his lawyer personally.

4. Ask the lawyer to advise you as to what you are entitled to in terms of marital assets and spousal maintenance (if any). If appropriate, ask for advice about child support and parenting arrangements for your children.

5. Ask about any other issue that you think might be relevant to your case.

6. If and only if the lawyer agrees to this, the best plan is to record the consultation on an audio device. If you're not permitted to record the conversation, you'll need to take notes. (It may be helpful for you to take a relative or friend with you to the meeting; they may be able to fill in any gaps in your notes or memory.)

7. Ask the lawyer to confirm their advice in a letter or email if possible.

At the end of this one-off consultation you should have a reasonably clear picture of where you stand. You will know approximately what share of the marital assets you are legally entitled to and whether or not you are entitled to spousal maintenance. If applicable, you will also have a good understanding of the arrangements for the care of children that divorcing parents are required by law to make.

Armed with this valuable information and advice, you can now approach negotiations with your ex or his lawyer with a considerable degree of confidence. So, if your ex makes unreasonable or unfair proposals to settle your legal issues, you can reject them in the knowledge that the position you are taking is fully supported by the law.

Don't under any circumstances represent yourself in negotiations with your ex or his lawyer if you don't know precisely what your legal rights are. That would be a recipe for disaster. You need to be smarter than that.

If the process of negotiation fails to resolve your legal issues and, based on the expert legal advice you've received, you believe that your husband is acting unreasonably and that his legal position is untenable, you have one remaining avenue of enforcing your legal rights, but it's not for the faint of heart. You will need to go to court without legal representation and ask a judge to make a decision about all the disputed issues in your case. In this scenario you would be known as a self-represented litigant.

Although it's your right to have your disputed legal issues resolved by a court of law, representing yourself in formal court proceedings is a demanding, stressful and daunting process and it's not for everyone. It's important to be aware of this. You will need to consider carefully whether the benefit to be gained by going to court outweighs the cost of the stress it may entail. Everyone's case is different, and this is a decision only you can make.

If, having weighed up the pros and cons, you decide that it is in your best interests to take your ex to court, your best bet is to make another one-off appointment with a family law expert to seek advice about the ins and outs of self-representation. For additional information and advice, try typing 'self-represented litigant family law (name of your country)' into an internet search engine. The court will also provide information to assist you (and the judge may allow you to bring a friend for support and to assist you with administrative tasks), but in the end you will be fully responsible for conducting your case and, equally, you will be responsible for the outcome.

Hang in there

Regrettably, even women who have retained a lawyer, and have been properly advised as to the minimum share of the marital assets they are entitled to, sometimes become so distraught by the process of settling the legal issues associated with the end of their marriage that they fall victim to the 'just get it over with' mindset – a common but unfortunate phenomenon in divorce cases. In this scenario women agree to accept a smaller share of the marital assets than they're entitled to so that they can put an end to the legal process, begin the process of recovery, and get on with their life. Many later regret that decision. Don't be one of them.

Stand firm

Obtaining expert legal advice following separation and asserting your rights in a determined manner is one of the best and most empowering decisions you'll ever make. Demand the legal settlement that you're entitled to – and don't falter. If necessary – but only after carefully evaluating the pros and cons – take your ex to court and have the matter dealt with fairly and squarely by a judge.

When you enforce your rights proactively, as advocated in this chapter, and you get the divorce settlement you're entitled to according to law, you begin your recovery from a position of strength and with a sense of accomplishment.

> ≫ *The minute you settle for less than you deserve, you get even less than you settled for.*
>
> **MAUREEN DOWD**
> AMERICAN COLUMNIST

CHAPTER 2

Smart Decisions, A Happier Life

>>> *It's our choices that matter in the end.
Not wishes, not words, not promises.*

ALEXANDRA BRACKEN
IN THE NOVEL *PASSENGER*

AFTER YOUR MARRIAGE has come to an end you'll find you are faced almost daily with decisions that need to be made, whether for yourself or, if you have dependent children, for your family. All of these decisions will require careful consideration, and some may significantly influence the quality of your life far into the future.

Making such decisions is never easy, but it becomes especially difficult at this time, when you're likely to be feeling distressed and emotionally fragile. The stress of separation and divorce can impair your capacity to think clearly and undermine your ability to make choices that are right for you. So, what's the best way forward? That's exactly what this chapter is about. Its purpose is to help you bring some order to the seeming chaos of your thoughts and increase your chances of making decisions that will be in your best interests.

Legal vs non-legal issues

Chapter 1 emphasises the importance of seeking advice from a lawyer before making decisions about any legal matters related to your divorce. But when it comes to non-legal issues, you have to take charge yourself. One of the best places to start is to familiarise yourself (or, as the case may be, reacquaint yourself) with the steps involved in making well-considered decisions. But first, let's look at some of the issues you're likely to be faced with.

Some common non-legal issues

Some of the most common non-legal questions women ask themselves both before and after they have separated from their husband are listed below. Not all will apply to you, and some will arise at different stages of your divorce process, depending on your individual circumstances.

- How will I tell my husband that I want a divorce?
- How will I explain to my children that their father and I are separating? What can I do to minimise their distress? What arrangements will need to be made to ensure they have regular, ongoing contact with both me and their father and continue to get the love, care and attention they were getting when we were all still together?
- Will I need professional counselling to cope with the divorce? What about my children?
- What kind of relationship do I want with my ex from now on? How much contact should we be having?
- Or, if appropriate: Now that there is so much bitterness between me and my ex, should I block him from being able to phone, text or email me? If I do that, how will we communicate if necessary?
- Which of our mutual friends should I confide in about the separation and the reasons why my husband and I have decided to get a divorce? (Remember that, depending on the circumstances of the divorce, mutual friends may feel they owe their loyalty to one partner rather than the other, often the partner they have known longer.)

- Should I stay in touch with my ex's family?
- What will I do about the friends or family members who have turned against me since the separation? Is it time to just let them go? If so, what's the best way of going about that?
- Should I revert to my maiden name?
- Do I need to return to the workforce?
- Should I return to the workforce even though I'm in a position to enjoy a reasonable standard of living if I don't?
- Should I enrol in a course of study to improve my employability or my prospects of earning a higher salary in my current job?
- Perhaps I should change my career altogether?
- Do I need to replace my car? If so, should I buy a brand-new car or a second-hand one?

A step-by-step approach to decision-making

Good decisions are simply decisions that you judge to be in your best interests or in the best interests of your children or of someone else who depends on you. When such decisions produce the result you had hoped for, they contribute to your overall well-being – or the well-being of your children or someone else – in a practical way, but also psychologically and emotionally. So, how do you maximise your chances of making good decisions?

While there are no guarantees, of course, the four-step process set out here is generally considered to be one of the approaches most likely to lead to a decision that will have the desired outcome.

1. Gather as much relevant information as you can. You are unlikely to make a good decision if you don't have all, or at least most of, the facts. Seek information online from

reliable sources, check out your local bookstore or library for relevant books, or talk things over with people you trust. Try to identify all your alternatives.

2. Think carefully about the issue and your options. Try to look at everything from all angles. For example, ask yourself what's likely to happen if you do X, and then ask yourself what's likely to happen if you don't do X, and so on. Once you've formed a preliminary view, it's a good idea to sleep on it.

3. Ask yourself: Does it feel right? Is it consistent with my values? If it doesn't feel right, try to identify exactly what's troubling you. Ask yourself what you may have overlooked. Perhaps you haven't thought the issue through thoroughly? Do you need to work through the process again?

4. Make your decision, put it into action, and accept that you've made the best decision you can in the light of your present knowledge and circumstances. That's all anyone can do.

Some helpful advice

The following tips may also be helpful:

- ▶ Where possible, avoid making major decisions in the immediate aftermath of separation when your emotions are running high. It's only natural to be concerned about the kind of future you want for yourself and your family, but it's wise to defer important decisions until you're in a position to think more clearly.

- ▶ Don't try to force a decision. Give yourself time. Things will become clearer in due course.

- Don't be influenced by what might please or displease your ex, your relatives or your friends. Put such thoughts aside and focus on what's right for you and, if appropriate, your children.

- However carefully you plan, not all your decisions will turn out as you may have hoped they would. That's life. Don't be hard on yourself if some things go awry. You can't know or control everything, and none of us has a crystal ball.

- If your circumstances permit, don't be afraid to take a risk. Perhaps it's time to take the road less travelled?

Once the four-step process begins to pay off for you, you will gain confidence in your ability to continue making decisions that will in most cases serve you well, now and long into the future. Try it and see.

>>> *Trust yourself. You know more than you think you do.*

BENJAMIN SPOCK
AMERICAN PAEDIATRICIAN

CHAPTER 3

Money, Money, Money

>>> *Balancing your money is the key to having enough.*

ELIZABETH WARREN
UNITED STATES SENATOR

WHILE SOME WOMEN are in a position to lead a comfortable, financially independent lifestyle after divorce, the reality for many women is vastly different. The financial challenges many women face after divorce can seem overwhelming, often requiring them to make a significant adjustment to their lifestyle and accept a drastically reduced standard of living. Some women's circumstances are so dire that they struggle to put food on the table and pay their bills, never mind trying to save for the future.

A wealth of good advice about personal money management is readily available from reputable sources on the internet and from money-management books written specifically for the average person by well-qualified finance writers. Some of the most commonly recommended ideas drawn from those sources are presented here. If making ends meet is proving to be a headache for you at the moment, the strategies outlined in this chapter may help to ease your worries and put you on the road to a more secure financial future.

The following are the most common reasons why many women find themselves struggling financially after divorce. One or more of these may apply to you.

- Going from a two-income household to only one income. The impact of the reduction in income will vary from woman to woman and will depend on such circumstances as whether she is working full-time, part-time or as a casual and whether her income alone is sufficient to support her and her family; whether her ex is paying her the appropriate amount of spousal maintenance and meeting his child support obligations (if applicable); and whether she received a just and equitable share of the marital assets.

- The value of the marital assets may have been very low. For example, you and your ex may have always lived in rented accommodation and may not have owned outright, or been paying a mortgage on, a home of your own. Similarly, you and your ex may not have acquired much in the way of personal property, such as furniture, cars, white goods or entertainment systems.

- You may have little or no money in the bank because you and your ex had next to no cash savings to be shared out at the time of separation.

- You may have sole custody of young children and no ready or affordable form of childcare, leaving you unable to work and reliant on government assistance for income. This problem will be compounded if your ex is not meeting his child support obligations.

- You may not have the physical or mental capacity to work.

- You may be able to work but be finding it difficult to obtain suitable employment.

- For any or all of the above reasons you may have little prospect of accumulating adequate funds for your retirement years or your old age.

▶ Your ex-husband may have been largely responsible for managing the family finances during the marriage, leaving you with limited experience of financial management.

Taking control of your finances is critically important at this time. It's one of the most constructive steps you can take towards establishing your independence and recovering from your divorce. To help you get started, some basic rules of money management are set out below.

Boost your financial IQ

The first step towards financial independence is to educate yourself about how to manage your money effectively. As noted at the beginning of this chapter, a wealth of information is readily available, much of it free. For example, you can search the internet (just type 'how to be financially independent' into a search engine), or you can buy, or borrow from your local library, some books about personal finances.

If you feel you need expert assistance in getting your finances under control, government social security departments and some religious and charitable organisations offer free, independent and professional financial counselling. Again, the internet can help you to locate an appropriate source of advice close to you. Eligibility criteria may apply, but if you qualify for free professional advice, this would be an excellent, and also the safest, starting point. You're free to decide how much of the advice to follow, of course, but you will almost certainly learn things that you wouldn't have discovered on your own. Crucially, you'll receive advice about such things as pensions, childcare subsidies and other forms of government assistance, all of which can be quite complex and difficult to research independently.

Develop a financial plan

Your next step is to develop a solid plan. Write down a list of your financial goals. It might look something like this:

- I want to increase my income.
- I want to reduce my living expenses.
- I want to provide a reasonable standard of living for myself and my children.
- I want to be able to pay my rent and utilities bills on time.
- I want to be debt-free.
- I want to accumulate some savings for emergencies and unexpected expenses.
- I want to maximise my eventual retirement or old age income.

Prepare a budget

A budget is simply a document that sets out your income and your expenses. If you're not sure how to put together a budget, you'll find plenty of templates by searching the internet. Many newsagents and stationery stores also sell inexpensive budget planners you can fill in by hand. Once you establish how much money is left over each week after meeting your living expenses, you'll know how much you can save for unexpected expenses and to invest for your future. If your expenses exceed your income, you'll need to make some radical changes, such as substantially reducing your expenditure or increasing your income, or both.

Increase your income

That sounds all very well, you may be thinking, but how do you do this? The following practical suggestions cover a wide range of options.

- ▶ First things first: Make sure that you're receiving all the financial and other assistance available to you under various government programs. Now that your circumstances have changed, you may be eligible for benefits and other forms of assistance you were not entitled to while you were married. Contact your government social security department to find out what applies in your situation. It's advisable to do this as soon as possible, as payments may be backdated to the date of your application, not to the date you separated from your ex.

- ▶ If you are employed, ask your employer for a raise (assuming you are able to make a good case for this) or more working hours. Alternatively, perhaps you can ask what you would need to do to qualify for promotion to the next level.

- ▶ Look for a part-time job with flexible starting and finishing times, such as driving for a ride-share operator.

- ▶ You may be able to work part-time or full-time as a domestic housecleaner, either independently or through an agency, but be sure to check out the legal and insurance requirements either way.

- ▶ If you like animals, you might consider setting up a dog-walking or animal day-care business, but take care to check out all the legal requirements first, including registration of the business.

- ▶ You may be able to earn money from home on your computer, tablet or smartphone. Type 'how to make money online' into an internet search engine and you'll find an abundance of companies that may pay you to provide feedback to their clients about your user experience of their websites and apps, or for your opinion about prototype products that their clients are working on. Just be aware that eligibility criteria may apply.

- Why not try mystery shopping? Again, information about this is readily available on the internet. But do some research and take care to register with a reputable company.

- Have a garage or car-boot sale.

- If you have a flair for cooking, you could start up a business baking custom-made cakes for special occasions (or something else likely to be in demand). You could market your new venture by setting up a social media business page, by selling your fare at markets, fetes and festivals, or by advertising in school newsletters. Or you may have some other skill you can earn money from.

Reduce your living expenses

Whether or not you manage to increase the amount of money coming in, it's worth investigating ways you can cut down on the amount of money going out. Check out the following ideas:

- If you have multiple personal debts such as credit cards, store cards or bank loans, speak to your bank or finance company about refinancing them all into a single loan with one, more manageable, monthly repayment.

- Enquire at your bank or credit union about the range of credit cards on offer. Some offer a no-frills, low-fee credit card that you may find better suits your needs.

- Compare the fees charged by your utilities providers (electricity, gas, water and so on) with those of other companies. Some government departments or agencies provide comparison charts on their websites. You may find a better deal.

- Instead of driving your car, use public transport or ride your bike where possible. (This may also reduce your car insurance premium, if you have insurance.)

▶ If you are on a low income, or if you hold the relevant type of government-issued pension card, you may be entitled to discounts on a wide range of products and services. So, be sure to check with retailers or service providers as to what discounts are available to people in your situation before you make any purchases or sign up to a service provider. Services and products that may be available to you at a lower cost include:

— Visits to a doctor or dentist

— Consultations with specialist healthcare providers

— Prescription medicines

— The hire of a wide range of mobility aids or medical equipment

— Ambulance fees

— Hearing testing

— Prescription eyeglasses

— Haircuts

— If you have a car or some other type of vehicle: government registration fees, the fee for obtaining or renewing your driver licence, the fee for roadside assistance programs, premiums on insurance policies, and mechanical maintenance and repairs for your car or other vehicle

— Utilities bills (electricity, gas, water and so on)

— Bank account fees

— Home and contents insurance

— Public transport

— Court filing fees

— Mail redirection

- Council or shire rates, or property taxes. (The names and nature of these council or government levies vary between countries.)

- ▶ Make a list of the groceries you need each week and stick to it. Buy generic brands; where possible, shop at markets close to closing time; and try not to shop on an empty stomach. If you buy your groceries regularly from a chain store, consider signing up to its customer loyalty program. The savings and other benefits available to members of such programs can be well worthwhile.

- ▶ Wait for end of season sales before buying more expensive items.

- ▶ Take your lunch to work.

- ▶ Buy pre-loved. Remember, it doesn't have to be new to be perfect for you.

- ▶ If you're going to the cinema, go on discount days.

Plan for unforeseen bills

Expecting the unexpected is a part of life for everyone, no matter what their financial circumstances may be. So, if this is feasible in your case, arrange to have a modest percentage of your weekly income (from whatever source) paid automatically into a separate savings account. What you don't see, you don't miss. These savings will serve as an emergency fund to help pay for those unexpected short-term expenses that can crop up from time to time, such as the cost of urgent medical treatment, replacing a worn-out home appliance, or necessary maintenance on your car, if you have one. Everyone's situation is different, but as a guide you might aim to have between $500 and $1000 in your emergency fund at all times. Even if you can save only $10 each week, you'll have $520 at the end of the year.

If you're concerned about possible crises that may arise in the future and cause financial headaches for you over a longer period of time (such as losing your job or being ill for an extended period), it's a wise move to accumulate enough in your emergency fund to cover all your expenses for up to three months.

But if you receive a government benefit or some other form of assistance and an unexpected expense crops up at a time when you don't have an emergency fund (or the balance of your fund is insufficient to cover the expense), you may be entitled to an advance payment on your benefit. If this situation arises, you should contact the relevant government department without delay.

Your emergency fund provides a financial buffer zone, reducing the likelihood that you'll need to borrow money when unforeseen expenses or life crises crop up. The key is to make a start and to continue making regular contributions until you have reached your goal. (Once you've done that, it's a good idea to investigate other options for investing any surplus money you are able to put aside.)

Save for your future

Many women's financial plan will include the goal of accumulating adequate funds for their retirement years (if they are employed) or their old age. If this applies to you, consider arranging to have a percentage of your weekly or monthly income (depending on what you can afford) paid into your superannuation fund as an additional contribution. (Author's note: This applies in Australia. Readers elsewhere might need to invest in a similar special-purpose fund to achieve this aim.)

Having adequate money for your needs gives you options. And when you have options, you are in the driver's seat of your own life.

>>>   *It takes as much energy to wish as it does to plan.*

ELEANOR ROOSEVELT
FORMER FIRST LADY OF THE UNITED STATES

CHAPTER 4

Proven Ways to Avoid Arguments

>>> *I don't have to attend every argument I'm invited to.*

W. C. FIELDS
AMERICAN COMEDIAN

MANY WOMEN, especially those who don't share the care of children, may have no need to have any contact with their ex after all the legal aspects of their divorce have been finalised. But if you do need to stay in contact with your ex and you tend to wind up in a heated quarrel every time you speak or exchange messages with him, you'll need to take a new approach to your interactions if you want to avoid years of torment.

The key thing to remember when you're in regular contact with your ex in a high-conflict divorce is to accept that you can't change him. You have no control whatsoever over what he thinks, says, writes in an email or in a text message, or does (short of your obtaining a protection order if warranted); you only have control over how you act and react. By adopting the following proven strategies, you can dramatically change the dynamics of your interactions in your favour.

- ▶ If you're nervous, try employing a relaxation technique before each interaction, even if it's just taking a few deep breaths.

- ▶ Avoid any contact with your ex that isn't absolutely necessary. If the last few interactions have gone smoothly, you might be tempted to contact him about an issue that's insignificant in the scheme of things – don't. You need to preserve your emotional equilibrium, and any exposure to him puts you at risk.

- Timing is everything. You know him well, so when is the best time to contact him so that you're more likely to catch him in a good mood?
- Face-to-face interactions are the riskiest. Go for a phone call, a text message or an email where possible.
- If you have to meet him in person, keep it brief. And be aware of your body language. Try to adopt a relaxed and composed stance. Remember to avoid crossing your arms, as this is a classic sign of defensiveness and will make you look less confident.
- Be prepared for every encounter. Write an agenda for each meeting or phone call that has the potential to be difficult, and stick to it. There's no need to show it to him – it's just for you.
- Decide what it is you want and ask for it clearly. Keep your conversations businesslike. Get quickly to the point, deal with it, and then politely terminate the conversation. By communicating with your ex in an efficient, structured and pragmatic way, you are adopting a non-threatening style, so he is much less likely to go on the offensive.
- Words matter, so try to avoid saying things like 'That's stupid' or 'Don't be so ridiculous'. If you agree with him about something, say so. The calming effect on your ex of hearing you say 'You're absolutely right about that. I totally agree' will surprise you.
- Don't dictate a solution – offer a suggestion.
- Don't focus on who's right and who's wrong – concentrate on resolving the conflict, perhaps by seeking a compromise.

- Try lowering your voice and speaking softly – he'll have to really concentrate on what you're saying. He's also likely to lower his own voice and slow his speech.

- Don't, under any circumstances, try to have a meaningful interaction with your ex if either of you is affected by alcohol.

- Name-calling doesn't help. Even if you're thinking 'You idiot', say 'I'm sure we can work this out'. It may not be easy for you to do this, but it's the smart move.

- If he's in merciless venting mode, say nothing until he's exhausted. Walk away if you have to, or terminate the phone conversation in a non-confrontational way, such as by saying calmly 'I have to go now'.

- Keep your private life private. Tell your ex the bare minimum, and if you have a new partner, don't bring your partner to any of your meetings.

Your ex will tend to treat you in the way you allow yourself to be treated, so it's imperative that you set boundaries and let him know clearly what they are. Remember your human rights. Don't tolerate abuse of any kind. You're not a doormat, so don't allow yourself to be treated like one.

Learning the art of communication in a high-conflict divorce takes time. Inevitably there will be an element of trial and error. Don't blame yourself if using these strategies doesn't always work. Any improvement at all is a victory for you.

>>> *The best armour is to keep out of range.*
ITALIAN PROVERB

CHAPTER 5

*Your Children Come First:
Making a Success of Shared Parenting*

>>> *Co-parenting ... It's a collaboration of parents doing what is best for the kids.*

HEATHER HETCHLER
US AUTHOR AND SPEAKER

IF YOU ARE A MOTHER, you will be deeply concerned as to how your divorce will affect your children, particularly young children. You will undoubtedly want to do whatever you can to minimise their unease or distress. The good news is that by understanding the different ways divorce affects children, and by following a few widely accepted shared parenting guidelines that have been proved over the years to be very effective, you can keep complications to a minimum and protect your children from unnecessary anguish.

How to tell your children

While this is bound to be a difficult conversation to have, some thought and careful planning will go a long way towards making it easier for you, your ex and your children. The news that their parents are separating will affect children differently, according to their age, their personality and their stage of development. If your children are very young and you are seriously concerned about how they will respond and how best to handle the situation, you may find it helpful to consult a child psychologist before you have the conversation. A psychologist who practises in this area will be able to offer advice as to the best way for you and your ex to comfort them should they become overly distressed and the most appropriate and sensitive way of answering their questions.

The following general guidelines may be helpful when telling your children about the divorce, whatever their ages.

- Jointly tell your children about your decision to end the marriage, but only if you and your ex can present as calm, rational and unified in your decision.

- Tell your children when they are all together if possible.

- Keep your explanation for the divorce as simple as you can.

- Tell your children about the divorce before you actually separate. This will allow time for you and your ex to discuss with them any concerns they may have as to how the divorce will affect the family unit, both in emotional terms and in practical ways. It will also give your children time to begin coming to terms with their parents' decision to separate, and for your children to foresee and prepare themselves for the life changes they will need to contend with in the future.

- Since your children may need to be comforted after the conversation, and may have many questions for you, try not to have the conversation just before taking them to school or putting them to bed.

How your children may be affected

As noted above, many factors influence children's experience of divorce, including their age, their personality and their level of development. Just three of the major difficulties most children have to negotiate at this time are: adjusting to and coping with the collapse of the family unit; not spending time with both parents every day; and becoming accustomed to living in two households. As a result, children may feel confused, they may feel rejected by the parent who leaves the family home, or they may harbour feelings of guilt, thinking that they may have caused or contributed to the separation. Such feelings often manifest in behaviour that is out of character, such as:

- Irritability
- Misbehaviour
- Separation anxiety
- Clinginess
- Difficulty in sleeping
- Nightmares
- Social withdrawal.

If you have any concerns about the severity or duration of your children's reaction to your separation it would be sensible to seek the advice of a suitably qualified psychologist.

Children have rights, parents have responsibilities

Children have a right to be happy and to grow up in an atmosphere of love, care and understanding. They benefit greatly when both their parents have a meaningful involvement in their lives, and they have a right to regularly spend time with, and communicate with, both of their parents as well as with any other people who play a significant role in their care, welfare and development, such as grandparents and other relatives. These rights exist regardless of whether their parents are married, separated or divorced, and you and your ex are equally responsible for ensuring that your children's rights are respected. There are, of course, exceptions to this general rule, such as when it is necessary to protect children from physical or psychological harm resulting from being subjected to, or exposed to, abuse, neglect or domestic violence.

These fundamental rights, and the principle that both parents have a duty to uphold them, are enshrined in the United Nations Convention on the Rights of the Child (UNCRC). According to the United Nations website, this treaty is 'the most rapidly and widely ratified international human rights treaty in history'.

Shared parenting after divorce

In the spirit of the rights formally recognised in the UNCRC, the best shared parenting arrangements are those that are child-focused. Such arrangements are designed to insulate the children as far as possible from the effects of any traumas their parents may be going through. They also ensure that the children spend time with all family members, and they establish a routine that reduces the risk that the children will witness any hostility. It's not about what suits you and your ex-husband; the overriding factor when parents make joint decisions about the long-term care, welfare and upbringing of their children after a divorce is that the children's best interests always come first.

The do's and don'ts of shared parenting

With these considerations in mind, let's look at some of the approaches to shared parenting that have been proved to minimise children's feelings of distress during and after a divorce. For precisely that reason, they are widely accepted as 'best practice' by child psychologists.

Do:

- Spend time with your children regularly and continue to show them love and affection and to give them your attention. Tell them often that the fact that you and their father are getting divorced in no way changes the love that both of you feel for them. You both love them just as much as you did before.

- Continue to show interest in their day-to-day lives by asking them about things such as school, friendships, sport and the various activities in which they're involved.

- Listen to your children attentively if they ask you why you and your ex decided to separate, and reassure them that you understand why they want to know. Tell them that divorce is very common but don't discuss the reasons for the separation in too much detail. Make certain they understand that the divorce is in no way their fault, then move on to another topic of conversation reasonably quickly or engage them in an activity.

- Explain to them that divorce doesn't mean that there is anything unusual or bad about their parents or their family.

- Reassure them that they don't have to choose between their parents. Tell them that although you and their father have decided not to be together any more, you will always be their parents and will work together as a team.

- Tell your children about the enjoyable and positive things you did while they were spending time with their father. This will help to reassure them that you're coping OK with the divorce, even when they're not with you.

- Continue to mention the children's father in general conversation from time to time and downplay any acrimony between you and your ex. While your children have to know ahead of the event that their parents are getting divorced, if the split is a bitter one there's no need for them to know this. So, it's OK for you to act as if you and their father are getting along well in the circumstances. In fact, it's not only acceptable to do this but also highly recommended if you want to give your children the best chance of adjusting to the new situation with as little upheaval as possible.

You might try asking them occasionally about their father in a caring way, or commenting on the fun they had the last time they were with him. Even if this is difficult for you, it will significantly relieve any feelings of anxiety your children may have as a result of having sensed or witnessed ill will between their parents on occasion, so it's well worth the effort.

- Involve them in discussions about the proposed shared parenting arrangements if they are of an appropriate age to understand such things. (This age is generally considered to be about 12.) Explain to them in detail how the shared parenting arrangements will work, but try to use simple language and sound positive. Shared parenting routines for children younger than 12 may be better formulated after you and your ex have discussed the matter with an appropriately qualified professional. If you and your ex haven't yet established what the shared parenting routine will be, it's OK to tell your children that you haven't yet decided but that there's no need for them to be concerned, as you and their father will work it out together.

- Provide them with consistent and predictable routines.

- Inform anyone who plays a significant role in your children's lives of the separation as soon as practicable after it has taken place.

- Make an appointment – preferably jointly with your ex – to meet with or talk on the phone to the principal of the children's school or childcare centre and the children's teachers or carers. Ask the principal, teachers and other staff to please keep a close eye on the children and to alert you to any warning signs of distress.

- Keep changeovers brief, and try to exchange a few friendly words with your ex in front of the children.
- Consider the likely longevity of a new relationship before involving your partner significantly in your children's lives. Children can become emotionally attached to a new partner quickly and profoundly.
- Be patient with your children. They will need time to adjust to their complex new family structure.
- Make it your overarching goal in respect of your children, regardless of their ages, to reassure them that their parents are a team and will jointly handle all aspects of the post-divorce parenting. This will help to relieve any stress or uncertainty they may be feeling and allow them to focus on their day-to-day child-appropriate activities.
- Consider taking your children to a child psychologist if you have serious concerns about their psychological or emotional state.

Don't:

- Speak unkindly about your ex to your children. (Whatever your private thoughts, remember what's in your children's best interests.)
- Unjustly hinder your children from spending time with their father.
- Allow your children to witness any unpleasant in-person exchanges between you and their father, or to read any nasty text messages or emails.
- Say anything to your children that might suggest to them you blame their father for the grief you may be feeling.

- Make your children your counsellor. If, for example, you seek comfort or advice from your children after you've had an argument with your ex, you place an unnecessary emotional burden on them. To do so would be contrary to the overarching goal of shielding your children from the potentially damaging psychological and emotional effects of the family breakdown.

- Discuss legal issues with your children.

- 'Pump' the children for information about their father.

- Use the children to pass messages to their father about contentious issues.

- Do changeovers at a police station. If changeovers don't take place at your respective homes, meet at an official contact centre, or at a neutral and pleasant venue, such as a park or the children's favourite fast food outlet.

Most children are more resilient than you may think. If the children of separated or divorced parents continue to be loved and cared for by both parents, they can deal with just about any family upheaval. The right kind of shared parenting gives them the best possible chance of growing up to be happy, healthy, well-adjusted adults who are free to achieve their full potential.

>>> *Kids would rather be from a broken home than live in one.*

DR PHIL
CLINICAL PSYCHOLOGIST AND TALK SHOW HOST

CHAPTER 6

Make Self-Care a Priority

>>> *Simple kindness to one's self and all that lives is the most powerful transformational force of all.*

DAVID R. HAWKINS
AMERICAN PSYCHIATRIST

SEPARATION, DIVORCE and adjusting to life after divorce are major life events. Both emotionally and physically, they demand a great deal of you. So, it's not just advisable to take good care of yourself at this time, it's essential – starting right now. Remember, even if you have dependent children or a responsibility to support someone else, you owe it to yourself and to those around you, especially your loved ones, to take good care of yourself. When you make time for calm, for silence, and for enjoyable activities that 'take you out of yourself', you energise your body and nourish your spirit.

Taking good care of yourself means attending to all your needs – physical, emotional and spiritual. This kind of self-care, sometimes called self-nurturing, has nothing to do with selfishness but is a vital part of the recovery process. It adds greatly to your overall well-being, restoring much-needed vitality and balance to your life.

Looking after yourself doesn't always require a lot of time. Whether it's ten minutes a day or all day on Sunday, the most important thing is that your body, mind and spirit get what they need. For example, maybe you need some solitude? Maybe you need the company of friends or particular family members? Maybe you need some retail therapy (finances permitting)? Maybe you need to run a marathon or to sleep for fourteen hours? Maybe you just need a warm hug? Whatever it is, the next step is to take whatever action is needed to make it happen.

Block out some time to do something you like doing on your own, whether it's a walk along the beach or settling down for a good read. Pick up the phone and ask your sister or a good friend if you can drop around, or arrange a coffee date. Book in for a massage. You get the idea.

There are so many ways to take care of your mind, body and soul at this time. Here are some more suggestions:

- Eat healthy, nutritious food in sensible quantities, at least most of the time.
- Try drinking chamomile tea. It's widely recommended for its calming effects.
- Get plenty of physical activity.
- Maintain good standards of personal hygiene and grooming.
- Ditch perfectionism.
- Try meditation. Information about classes and do-it-yourself techniques is readily available online.
- Seek the company of friends who cheer you up and make you laugh. Laughter triggers the release of endorphins, the body's natural feel-good chemicals. Endorphins relieve symptoms of low mood, promote a sense of well-being and can even temporarily relieve pain.
- If your finances permit, treat yourself to a facial or a pedicure, or maybe you'd prefer a massage, a spa or a sauna.
- Indulge in some aromatherapy.
- Sign up for a class in Pilates, yoga or tai chi.

- Take up an absorbing hobby. There's a wide variety of activities to choose from, and many can be learned online for free or by attending a modestly priced class. Why not try your hand at painting, drawing or photography; interior design; making jewellery or candles; flower arrangement; patchwork and quilting; or cake decorating, to mention just a few. Or you might enjoy learning a musical instrument, a new language or a style of dancing you haven't tried before.

- If you enjoy wine, joining a wine-tasting group can be a great way to spend relaxing time with friends or to make new friends.

- If you're the active type, consider doing something adventurous and challenging like tandem hang-gliding, open-water kayaking or rock-climbing.

- Sleep under the stars.

Give to yourself and do it now. It's time to apply your capacity for nurturing others to yourself as well.

> ⟩⟩⟩ *A good laugh and a long sleep are the best cures in the doctor's book.*
>
> **IRISH PROVERB**

CHAPTER 7

Alone But Not Lonely

>>> *What a lovely surprise to finally discover how un-lonely being alone can be.*

ELLEN BURSTYN
AMERICAN ACTRESS

AFTER SEPARATION many women will either need or choose to live alone at some stage. Everyone's situation is different, but if this applies to you and you feel apprehensive about the prospect (for example, you may be moving to a different area and leaving behind some or even most of your previous social networks), the suggestions in this chapter may help to ease your concerns. (And many of these suggestions may be equally helpful for those who aren't planning to live alone.) First up, the important thing to remember is that just because you live alone, it doesn't follow that you have to be lonely.

Time spent alone is sometimes a welcome relief – a joy, even – but we all know that too much of it can be oppressive and lead to loneliness and unhappiness. Making the transition from the daily companionship of marriage to living alone is rarely easy, but you will find below some tried-and-true strategies to help you negotiate the change as successfully and productively as possible.

- ▶ Keep in touch with the people who care about you and want to help – be they family members, friends, neighbours or acquaintances. You'll know who they are. Let them help.

(But if you should start to feel somewhat overwhelmed, feel free to let people know that, as much as you appreciate their kindness, you are managing OK but will ask for their help if you need it.)

- Remember that finding someone to share your accommodation, or moving in with someone else, is always an option for the future. (This would also help to reduce your living expenses.)

- If, for whatever reason, you are feeling somewhat adrift socially, which is not uncommon after divorce (also for those who aren't living alone), take steps to start building a new social network. Many people will tell you that it's one of the most rewarding things they did after the end of their marriage. If your future life is to be as fulfilling as you would like it to be, it's wise to cultivate a new network of friends and acquaintances who get to know you and accept you in your new circumstances. Doing some voluntary work; joining a fitness group or sporting club; taking a class in one of the creative arts or crafts or whatever else interests you; or perhaps joining a church community are all potentially good ways to get you started. This may require some courage at first, and not everything you try may prove to be a good fit for you, but you won't regret it.

- Think about getting a pet. Cats are low maintenance and good company. Dogs require more looking after and regular walks, but provide more affection and companionship than some people do! Or you may feel that birds or tropical fish are more your style.

- One of the best ways of warding off loneliness is to distract yourself, so when lonely or troubling thoughts threaten, try to keep busy. Take your dog for a walk, throw yourself into the housework, go shopping (or window shopping) or visit your local library. There are lots of options.

- If sleeping by yourself proves to be a problem, buy yourself a full-length, figure-hugging body pillow – you may be surprised at the difference it makes.

- Special occasions such as wedding anniversaries, Christmas Day, birthdays and other significant dates formerly spent with your ex can be difficult, so make plans ahead of time to do something that will take your mind off them. It's natural to think of them, but don't allow yourself to dwell on them.

It's interesting to note that it's becoming more and more common for women who have entered into a new long-term relationship – both women who are divorced and those who have separated from a long-term partner to whom they were not married – to choose to keep their own home and live on their own rather than move in with their new partner. There are many reasons for this, and (like most things) it's not for everyone, but it often proves to be a good arrangement for both parties. While this is not your current situation, it may provide you with food for thought as you embark on this new stage of your life.

Living alone undoubtedly has its benefits. For example, you can:

- Stay in bed all day if you feel like it.
- Eat what and when you like.
- Do housework only when you want to.
- Play whatever music you feel like listening to.
- Watch whatever films or series you want (whether on a DVD, via an online streaming service or at the cinema).
- Stay up as late as you want.
- Sleep more peacefully without a snoring companion.

Once you overcome your initial anxiety about living alone, you'll most likely find that it has many benefits you were previously unaware of. You'll have the freedom to indulge in some or all of the perks listed above; to develop new interests; and to keep in touch with family and long-established friends while also building new social networks. And at those times when you feel the need for some solitude, you may make the delightful discovery that you feel completely content with your own company. As famous English historian and writer Edward Gibbon once observed, 'I was never less alone than when by myself'.

> ⟫ *It's like magic. When you live by yourself, all your annoying habits are gone!*
>
> **MERRILL MARKOE**
> AMERICAN AUTHOR

CHAPTER 8

Domestic Violence – How to Protect Yourself and Your Family

>>> *There's a special place in hell for men who abuse women.*

ERIC GONDWE
AUTHOR AND CO-FOUNDER OF THE UNIVERSITY
OF EAST AND SOUTHERN AFRICA

VIOLENCE AGAINST WOMEN is rife all around the world. It's a despicable form of abuse that tramples on some of the most fundamental of women's natural rights, not to mention their legal rights as well. It's estimated that the majority of women know, or know of, someone who has been affected by this kind of abuse. After separation and divorce, most men cope without turning to aggressive behaviour, but a significant minority vent their anger, shock and sadness by going on the attack – literally. If you are unfortunate enough to be dealing with a violent or abusive ex, your life is probably a living hell. This chapter has been written for you.

What constitutes domestic violence?

Domestic violence now encompasses a wide array of abusive behaviours, because the nature of this scourge has evolved to include a broad range of conduct beyond the use of physical force. In many cases, domestic violence is a criminal offence.

The legal definition of domestic violence varies from jurisdiction to jurisdiction, but it may include any behaviour that is:

- Physically abusive
- Verbally abusive
- Sexually abusive
- Psychologically abusive
- Emotionally abusive
- Financially abusive
- Controlling or dominating
- Threatening.

The kinds of behaviour on your ex's part that may constitute domestic violence include the following:

- Causing you, your children, another member of your family, or a pet physical injury
- Threatening to injure or kill you, your children, someone else, or a pet
- Threatening suicide
- Vandalising your home or damaging your personal belongings
- Pressuring you to have sex
- Unlawfully stalking you
- Repeatedly phoning you, sending text messages or MMS messages to you, emailing you or contacting you via your social media account(s) without your consent
- Frequently shouting or using profane language during conversations with you or with any member of your family

- Attempting to convince you that you are insane (often called gaslighting)
- Withholding, or threatening to withhold, spousal maintenance or child support so as to control or dominate you.

The harmful consequences

Apart from the obvious bodily injury caused by physical assaults, domestic violence can be profoundly damaging to your psychological and emotional well-being and that of your children and other family members. One of the most tragic consequences of the ongoing violence and abuse that many women suffer during their marriage, or after separation or divorce, is that some of them begin to believe that they are somehow to blame. After years of having their self-worth relentlessly eroded, they feel that they don't deserve to be treated any better. Domestic violence and abuse are unacceptable in any circumstances – there is no excuse whatsoever for this kind of behaviour. You are not to blame for your ex-husband's conduct – it is his responsibility, and his alone.

How to protect yourself and your family

If you, any member of your family, or a pet is at risk of experiencing domestic violence or abuse of any kind – especially, but not only, if domestic violence has previously been an issue in your relationship – you should seek help without delay. This cannot be overstated. But it's also important to be aware of the steps that you personally can take to protect yourself and your family and to minimise the risk of harm in the future. The most effective ways of doing this are listed below.

- Contact the police immediately if your physical safety, or that of any family member or pet, is at risk. It would be wise to keep a record of your complaint (and any future complaints, should more than one be necessary), including the time and date and the names of the investigating officers.

▶ Similarly, tell your lawyer about any such threat. If you don't have a lawyer, Chapter 1 provides advice as to how to find one who specialises in family law and also explains the options available to you for avoiding upfront fees and for obtaining free legal services.

▶ Consider obtaining a restraining order. If you have a lawyer, your lawyer may prepare the necessary court documents, arrange to have them served on your ex, and obtain a date for a court hearing. Alternatively, your lawyer may refer you directly to the police, who handle domestic violence matters on a daily basis and are highly experienced in this area. This has the added advantage of saving you legal fees.

The restraints likely to be imposed on your ex by a protection order will depend on your particular circumstances. They may prohibit him from having any contact with you or members of your family, or may oblige him to stay a certain distance away from you and your family. If your ex breaches the protection order, he may be charged with a criminal offence and convicted. If you obtain a protection order, it would be advisable for you to provide a copy to your lawyer, to your ex's lawyer, to your family and to any dependable neighbours.

▶ Change your contact details as appropriate. This may involve:

— Redirecting your paper mail to the address of a trustworthy friend or to a Post Office box.

— Changing the password(s) for your existing email account(s) and, if you haven't already done so, activating two-step verification. (Information and advice about creating passwords that are virtually unbreakable are readily available on the internet.)

- Opening a new email account and redirecting all email from your old account(s) to the new one.

- Blocking your ex from sending emails to any of your email accounts, old and new.

- Changing the password(s) on your social media account(s) and blocking your ex from sending you messages via those platforms.

▶ Should it become necessary to conceal your location from your ex, remember to suppress your name and address from any publicly accessible government or other register on which those details are discoverable. Such registers may include the electoral roll(s) in any electorate(s) in which you are registered to vote.

▶ Carry a fully charged phone (preferably a smartphone) with you at all times, and keep the phone number for your local or regional domestic violence crisis line stored on the phone, as well as other relevant emergency numbers such as police, ambulance and fire brigade.

▶ Configure the settings on your phone so that your ex is unable to call you or to send text messages or MMS messages to you. (If he begins calling you or sending messages to you from a different phone number, you'll need to think about applying for a new phone number.)

▶ Keep, and also make copies of, all digital and 'hard copy' communications from your ex (or from anyone who has contacted you on his behalf) that cause you to be concerned that you, a member of your family, or a pet may be at risk of physical harm. Such communications may include text messages, MMS messages, emails, messages sent via your social media account(s), letters, and handwritten or typed notes on pieces of paper. Should it become necessary for you to contact the police or to apply to a court for a protection order, these communications may constitute compelling evidence of the risk posed by your ex.

There is a variety of ways to make copies of text messages and MMS messages. You'll find instructions for the various options on the internet. Just type in 'how to back up or print messages on a smartphone'. If your phone isn't a smartphone, you'll need to go 'old school' by placing your phone face down on a photocopier.

Because you may deliberately or inadvertently delete a relevant text message or MMS message from your smartphone before you've made a copy of it, it would be sensible to install an app on your phone or on your computer that allows you to recover any such deleted messages. Just type 'how to recover deleted messages from a smartphone' into an internet search engine. This should produce a list of apps that will be suitable for your purposes. (It's important to be aware that apps of this kind may only recover messages sent to your phone after the app has been installed, so it makes sense to install the app as soon as possible, before you need it.)

- Keep a whistle in your handbag.
- Keep a flashlight in your car and under your bed.
- Choose a trusted neighbour whom you can confide in about the risks you're facing, and tell them that if they have reason to believe you or your family are in danger, they should contact the police but never intervene and put themselves at risk.
- Organise a safe place you and your children can go to at very short notice if necessary. This might be the home of a trusted friend or the nearest women's refuge. If your children feel threatened by your ex-husband, have a frank discussion with them about safety. Tell them about the safety measures you've put in place, and that you've

organised a secure place you can take them to should the need arise – a place where they will be perfectly safe whether or not you're able to stay there with them. (Exactly how and how much you tell them will obviously depend on their ages.)

- Pack an emergency suitcase (preferably one with wheels) or overnight bag with a few essentials so that you can leave your home at very short notice if necessary. If you have children, pack a lightweight bag (or bags) for them as well and keep the bags where they are readily accessible.

- If you own a pet that could be at risk if you had to leave your home suddenly, it would be wise to plan ahead and investigate what options there are for safeguarding it in your absence, at least temporarily, until help arrives. The police or your vet are likely to be able to suggest some practical strategies. But always remember that your safety and that of your children are paramount.

- If your ex has a key to your home, change the locks on the doors (and windows, if they have keyed locks) and keep them locked at all times, even when you're at home.

- Don't open the door unless you know who is outside. Install a peephole and a safety chain if they're not already in place.

- If you don't already have them, fit locks and safety screens to secure your windows; install sensor lights to detect movement outside windows and doors; and consider installing an alarm system in your home. If you can't afford these measures, phone a local security system provider (alternatively, your local council may be able to help) and ask whether any subsidy is available for low-income earners. If these kinds of protections are still beyond your means, check out the range of imitation surveillance cameras at your local electronics store. Modern 'dummy' surveillance cameras are not only inexpensive but also very realistic. Many have a battery-operated flashing red light to indicate to any would-be intruders that their movements are being recorded.

- ▶ Think about getting a dog with a strong protective instinct that will bark when a stranger approaches the home. (Many dogs have this instinct, but it's stronger in some breeds than others.) As well as alerting you, a barking dog can act as an effective deterrent. But before you take this step you need to do some research and seek advice from reliable sources (such as professional dog trainers, dog clubs and vets) to find out which breeds are most likely to suit you and your circumstances. It's also essential to inform yourself fully of both the practical issues involved in owning and training a dog and the legal requirements, including any related to owning a dog kept specifically to act as a watchdog. Your local council will be able to advise you.

- ▶ Consider whether counselling for you or your children would be helpful.

- ▶ Trust your intuition. If something doesn't feel right, it probably isn't.

If, despite having taken some or all of these precautions, you do become the victim of a domestic violence incident, your first course of action should be to report it to the police and to your lawyer without delay. In addition, it would be highly advisable for you to make detailed notes about the incident in a diary or notebook. Be precise. What happened? What day and time did the incident occur? Who said what to whom? Were there any witnesses? Did you seek medical attention? If so, where did you go and which doctor did you see? Take photos of any injuries or property damage. It's a good idea to make your notes as soon as practicable after the incident has occurred. This will increase the likelihood that your account will be accurate and include all the relevant details.

Domestic violence is a grievous infringement of your legal and human rights and can cause significant long-term damage to your health and that of your family. If you are a victim of this kind of behaviour, it's essential that you report it to the police and to your lawyer, if you have one, and to be proactive about taking steps to protect yourself and your loved ones in the future. Don't suffer in silence – if the campaign against this kind of abuse is to be effective, victims have to be willing to report it. And above all, remember that you're not alone – help is available.

> ⋙ *Life shrinks or expands in proportion to one's courage.*
>
> **ANAIS NIN**
> AMERICAN-CUBAN-FRENCH ESSAYIST

CHAPTER 9

*Same-Sex Divorce –
The Special Challenges*

〉〉〉 *A good half of the art of living is resilience.*

ALAIN DE BOTTON
SWISS-BORN BRITISH PHILOSOPHER AND AUTHOR

DIVORCE IS RARELY IF EVER SIMPLE, but for same-sex couples the end of a marriage potentially involves some unique legal complications and practical problems. Although the patterns of divorce for same-sex couples are understudied in comparison with those of heterosexual couples, it's already clear that same-sex couples who divorce are faced with a range of complex issues unique to their lifestyle and circumstances. Because of this, you may be vulnerable to severe forms of stress over and above those experienced by most of your heterosexual counterparts. This is particularly so in countries where same-sex marriage is a relatively new institution. (For the sake of clarity, same-sex marriage is the marriage of two people of the same sex or gender. So, in countries where same-sex marriage has been legalised, all members of the LGBTIQ community have the right to marry any other member of that community, subject to the prohibitions that apply to all marriages in that country.)

The special challenges

The unique difficulties that same-sex couples going through a divorce may encounter include those in the following list.

- The emotional trauma inherent in the end of a marriage may be compounded for some same-sex couples by two additional sources of stress: their exposure to prejudice in the form of homophobia or transphobia in their everyday life, and their awareness that same-sex marriages are often stigmatised. The combined effect of these life experiences can sometimes become overwhelming, severely eroding the resilience of one or both parties and leaving them more than usually vulnerable to mental health issues such as depression and anxiety.

- Because the LGBTIQ community has campaigned strenuously over many years for marriage equality, same-sex couples who decide to divorce may be susceptible to heightened feelings of embarrassment and failure.

- You may find that some members of your family and some of your heterosexual friends and work colleagues don't treat a same-sex divorce as a 'real' divorce. As a consequence, you may not receive as much support as you need. This problem will be even more profound if some of your heterosexual friends have shunned you or some members of your family have disowned you since you came out.

- If during the process of your divorce you feel you need the support of a suitably qualified counsellor or mental health professional, you may find there is a shortage in your local area of practitioners with an understanding of the challenges unique to same-sex divorces. If that proves to be the case, try searching the internet for 'LGBTIQ-friendly counselling near me'. Should it be impracticable for you to travel to meet your nearest therapist, many therapists offer counselling via a video conference. Many modern video conferencing services provide flawless video, crystal clear audio and reliable performance. They can create a virtual counselling environment that is surprisingly realistic, warm and friendly.

- If domestic violence is an issue in your divorce, you may be reluctant to call the police, fearing that the investigating officers may be homophobic or transphobic. A possible solution to this issue is set out in more detail below.

- In cases where a same-sex couple have become parents with the assistance of a third party, shared parenting arrangements after divorce can become a complicated issue. Given the significance of this topic, it is dealt with in more detail below.

- If you married in a country where same-sex marriage is legal and have subsequently relocated to a country where it isn't legal, you may not be able to get a divorce. In order to dissolve the marriage, it may be necessary for you or your ex-partner to establish residence in a place where same-sex marriage has been legalised.

- You may feel hesitant about seeking legal advice on virtually any issue because of concern that your lawyer may be homophobic or transphobic. See below for a solution to this problem.

- Because same-sex divorce is still a niche area of legal practice in some places, lawyers may need to dedicate more time to cases than they would when dealing with most heterosexual divorces, leading to higher legal fees.

Some shared parenting issues

When same-sex couples decide to become parents, the creation of the family necessarily involves a third party, such as a sperm donor, an egg donor, an embryo donor or a surrogate mother. That third party may have continuing contact with the child and may play a major role in the child's life.

To give just one example, this is quite common in cases where the third party is a sperm donor who had a close relationship with the birth mother and her partner before conception. If the marriage breaks down, this can lead to great distress for all concerned, including the child, and also to complicated disputes about how the parties will share the parenting of the child in the future. The problem may be compounded if the law in the jurisdiction in which the divorce is being dealt with is unclear as to the legal definition of 'parent' in sperm donor cases, raising complex legal issues which may have to be determined in court by a judge.

Same-sex couples may be understandably apprehensive at the prospect of having key parenting issues resolved under laws that are unclear, and they may also consider the court system to be inhospitable to them. Future changes to legislation may clarify these kinds of parenting issues, but this is likely to remain a complicated area. And because of the increasing number of same-sex divorces, the number of families involved in such parenting disputes will rise in the coming years.

Chapter 5 covers the do's and don'ts of shared parenting after divorce in considerable detail. The information in that chapter may provide you with some helpful tips as to how to put arrangements in place that not only are in the best interests of your child but that also minimise the potential for conflict between you, your ex and any third party about parenting-related issues.

Protect yourself from domestic violence

If you are unfortunate enough to have been the victim of domestic violence during your marriage – or if you have experienced it in a previous relationship and, seeing the warning signs, are concerned that it may become an issue during or after your divorce – it would be highly advisable to take steps to increase the likelihood that, should you require immediate police assistance, the attending officers will be LGBTIQ-friendly. Here's what to do.

Contact your local police station, whether by attending in person, by telephoning or by going online. Explain that you are going through a same-sex divorce and that you either have been the victim of domestic violence or have concerns that you may become a victim of domestic violence during or after your divorce, whichever is appropriate. Ask if the police station has an LGBTIQ liaison program in place to deal with LGBTIQ-related domestic violence issues. If so, they may be able to provide you with a list of the relevant liaison officers and their contact details.

In co-operation with governments, an increasing number of police stations are putting LGBTIQ liaison programs (or other comparable programs) in place. Under such programs, certain police officers are nominated as LGBTIQ liaison police. These police can provide support and assistance to members of the LGBTIQ community who are the victims (or potential victims) of domestic violence or who need to report other criminal behaviour.

If the police station doesn't have an LGBTIQ liaison program in place, ask if there are any other policies or procedures in place to ensure that, should an incident of domestic violence occur, the attending officers will be, at the very least, LGBTIQ-friendly. If you find there are no such policies or procedures in place, and you're concerned that in the event of your contacting the police to report a domestic violence attack by your ex – or to report that you are at imminent risk of an attack – you may be exposed to homophobic or transphobic discrimination on the part of the attending officers, it would be sensible to consider in advance what you will say when you call for help so as to reduce the likelihood of this.

What you say will depend on a number of factors, including your personality, the sex of the person who answers your emergency call, and the level of compassion that person may show in relation to domestic violence matters generally. If you feel you need some advice about how to handle this call, try calling one of the growing number of LGBTIQ support services. They will almost certainly be able to help you, or at least point you in the direction of someone else who can help. There is no right or wrong way to handle an emergency phone call such as this – it's entirely a personal decision. You may choose not to reveal that you are married to the perpetrator. Or you may feel that in the circumstances it seems like the right thing to do. Trust your intuition here. It's usually right in these kinds of situations.

Finally, if during or after your divorce you become the victim of a domestic violence incident involving your ex, or are in imminent danger of becoming a victim, it is of the utmost importance that you contact the police immediately, whether or not an LGBTIQ liaison program is in place in your area and whether or not you're concerned that the attending officers may not be LGBTIQ-friendly. In crisis situations such as these, the safest course of action is always to dial the emergency phone number in your country and request urgent police assistance. This recommendation is consistent with the strong advice given by law enforcement agencies around the world.

Meeting the challenges

So, given the potential difficulties and complications that may arise in the process of your divorce, where's the most constructive place to start? The answer is to start by doing two key things. These two things will not only set you on the path to minimising the stress inherent in the special challenges you may face when going through the divorce process but will also help to alleviate the emotional consequences of divorce and give you the best chance of putting the trauma behind you and rebuilding your life.

1. It's imperative to obtain expert legal advice from a lawyer who is conversant with same-sex divorce and sympathetic to the particular circumstances of same-sex couples. Such lawyers can be found by typing 'LGBTIQ (or same-sex) family lawyer near me' into an internet search engine or browsing through online and hard-copy LGBTIQ-friendly magazines. Many lawyers advertise their services in these magazines – look for the rainbow flag.

2. Don't be afraid to call on the people around you who understand the unique challenges faced by same-sex couples going through a divorce and who genuinely care about you and want to help you to recover and create a new life. The kindness, affection and encouragement of others are invaluable at this time. And if you feel that professional guidance – or simply a neutral person to talk things over with – would be helpful, don't hesitate to seek the advice of an appropriately qualified and experienced mental health professional or counsellor who specialises in LGBTIQ issues. There is no shame in seeking assistance of this kind – when it comes to divorce, everyone needs all the help they can get.

Looking to the future

The process of recovering from the trauma of divorce is in many respects the same for same-sex and heterosexual divorcees. So the advice given in Chapters 1–8 is likely to be equally helpful for both. No one can promise same-sex couples who are going through a divorce a smooth ride. But if you've followed the recommendations in this book – and, crucially, if you've taken the two key initiatives set out above – you will have gone a long way towards overcoming the unique difficulties you may face along the way and given yourself an excellent chance of rising to the challenges and moving on from one of life's most stressful experiences.

>>> *However long the night, the dawn will break.*
AFRICAN PROVERB

CHAPTER 10

Looking for Love Again

>>> *You can't close yourself off from love. I try to keep my heart open and not feel afraid.*

MIRANDA KERR
AUSTRALIAN MODEL AND AUTHOR

ONE OF THE MOST TELLING SIGNS that you've accepted that your marriage has ended and that you've detached yourself emotionally from your ex-husband is that you start looking for love again. So, what's the best way of 'getting back out there', as is often said? The dating scene has changed radically since the advent of the internet. While it's still possible, of course, to meet someone through mutual friends, sporting or other interests, or such activities as taking your dog to the park or shopping at your local supermarket, many women are finding that internet dating is a more realistic way to meet men. Online dating can be a lot of fun and can have the desired outcome, but it can also be time-consuming, stressful and frustrating. And since you may occasionally cross paths with men who will behave disrespectfully, it can also be upsetting. So, you need to decide what your own personal dating policies are going to be, and to stick to them.

How to get started

The rapid growth of online dating around the world has given rise to an ever-increasing demand from users for advice that will help them improve their experience of it and enhance their chances of success. This, in turn, has generated a wealth of practical and useful information on the internet, with numerous online feature articles and webpages now offering comprehensive guidance for anyone taking the plunge into cyber-dating. These resources are well worth a look. To help you get started, a selection of the most common and widely accepted online dating guidelines drawn from those resources is set out below. These guidelines will help you to attract the right kind of attention, avoid the wrong kind, and maximise your chances of finding someone compatible.

Choose a dating website that's right for you

If you're new to online dating, the task of finding a website or smartphone app that's a good fit for you can be quite bewildering. (For simplicity I'll refer to all internet dating services as apps.) The abundance and diversity of dating apps are staggering. Since choosing an app that you enjoy using and that is most likely to be successful for you may be the most important part of the internet dating process, it's well worth your while to do some research. Try typing 'best dating apps and websites near me' into an internet search engine. It's then simply a matter of clicking on the link to each app and browsing its home page to determine if it's likely to suit your needs. Your intuition is usually a good indicator here. Be guided by it.

Once you've registered with an app and have started browsing men's profiles and receiving messages, you may find that the app doesn't feel right for you. You may need to try several apps before finding one you like. Trial and error are an inevitable part of online dating, so it's common practice, and certainly sensible, to shop around for the right app.

Write an appealing profile

Your profile should portray the person you really are and be designed to attract the attention of the type of men you're looking for. So, don't try to please everyone – just be yourself. The following tips may be helpful:

- ▶ Remember that the sole purpose of your profile is to pique the interest of the kind of men you're trying to attract, so there's no need to tell your life story. Keep it brief (300 words is plenty) but inviting.

- ▶ A positive outlook on life is appealing, so aim to project an image of an optimistic woman who is looking forward to what the future holds. Negativity of any kind has no place in a dating profile.

- ▶ Most men find a sense of humour to be very appealing in women. And while everyone is different, most of us have a humorous side in one form or another, so consider incorporating yours into your profile. As long as it feels right to you, a touch of humour can go a long way towards attracting attention.

- ▶ Don't under any circumstances say anything that isn't true – dishonesty is a major turn-off and sooner or later you'll be caught out. To take an obvious example, if you lie about your age or your weight, this is bound to lead to embarrassment on your first date.

- ▶ Be clear about what kind of relationship you're seeking and what kind you're not.

- ▶ Be equally clear about your deal-breakers.

- ▶ List the values that are most important to you, but don't be overly prescriptive about the qualities you're looking for in a man or the kind of lifestyle you want him to lead. For example, avoid statements like 'Must love ballroom dancing and horse riding'.

- Avoid clichés such as 'I like hanging out with friends and family and going to barbecues' or 'I enjoy long walks on the beach in the moonlight'. You want to stand out from the crowd, so be genuine and original.

- Under no circumstances should you mention your ex or exes or give details of past relationships. It's a real turn-off.

- Never disclose personal information from which men browsing the app might be able to identify your surname, home address, phone number or workplace.

- Do a spell check.

- Ask a friend to review your profile before activating it.

A profile with photos attracts more attention

Uploading photos to your profile is generally not compulsory on dating apps, and for a variety of valid reasons many women choose not to do so. But if you're serious about finding someone, it's important for you to understand that many men will not initiate contact with a woman who hasn't posted photos. (And don't you prefer to see what the men you're thinking of contacting look like?) A well-chosen selection of photos that portray the real you is an integral part of the kind of profile that's likely to get the result you're hoping for. So, what's the best way of going about this?

You'll find a great deal of useful information on the internet to help you put together your photo gallery. Here's some of the advice most sources agree on:

- Four photos is about right, though this isn't a rigid rule. A variety of photos will obviously help to give the men who view your profile a more well-rounded sense of who you are and what you look like.

- Be sure to include at least one close-up shot of your face that shows you looking relaxed, approachable and happy with your life. This photo is usually the best choice for your main profile pic. The best approach is to keep it simple: look straight into the camera and smile naturally. A plain background such as a white brick wall usually works well. Don't apply a filter or post a so-called glamour shot. (Remember that the point of your profile photos is to show the real you.) While selfies are OK when composed properly, the unusual angle at which many are taken, and the sometimes-obvious outstretched arms, rarely produce a natural image of the kind you are aiming for. For the best result, ask a friend to take a few photos for you.

- Uploading at least two whole-body shots is strongly recommended. Most people (both men and women) don't want to see just a face; they want to see the whole body of someone with whom they're considering making contact. If you don't post any whole-body shots, many men will ask you to upload some anyway, so it's best to provide them up front. Good options for whole-body photos include outdoor scenes, such as standing on the shore of a beach, lake or river and leaning against a tree in a park. (For safety's sake, the background you choose should be unidentifiable.)

- Posting one or more photos that tell men a little more about your lifestyle is an excellent idea. A photo that shows you enjoying one of your favourite pastimes helps to form a picture of who you are and can really boost your appeal. (As noted above, make sure there is nothing in the photo that would allow someone to work out where you live or work or which places you're likely to frequent.)

- Be sure to post recent photos only, preferably photos taken within the last three months. (You'd be surprised how many people post photos that are up to ten years old.)

- If you don't have four recent photos that are suitable, you'll obviously need to arrange to have some taken. Since your photos are such an important part of your profile, it's well worth the effort. The simplest plan is to ask a friend to take some for you. (If you intend to have several taken on the one day, in different settings, remember that you'll need to take a few changes of clothes with you.)

- It may seem obvious, but don't include photos that show you wearing a hat and sunglasses. They mask your face, and men will obviously want to see clearly what you look like.

- All your photos should be properly focused. Blurry photos give the impression that you haven't put much effort into creating your profile or don't care about how you present yourself. And since the camera on most modern smartphones is usually of a high quality, taking photos that are clear and sharp is relatively straightforward.

- Don't include photos in which you're seen from a distance.

- If the photo includes other people, add a caption or mark that identifies you.

- If you're fond of animals and own a pet, it's a nice idea to include a pic of the two of you together.

- Needless to say, it would be completely unacceptable to post a photo of you and your ex in which he hasn't been completely cropped out.

Screen everyone carefully

If your profile attracts a very large number of responses, this may be due to what could be called the 'click from pic' approach to online dating. It's important to be aware of this. Many men only look at the photos women post and don't bother reading any further, so you may receive numerous messages from men with whom you are obviously incompatible. This can be a frustrating experience, especially if your profile clearly sets out your deal-breakers and specifies the type of man you're hoping to meet. It's a common problem, and one that women regularly and justifiably complain about in online forums.

Whether or not your profile attracts a lot of messages, careful vetting of anyone who contacts you (or anyone you're considering initiating contact with) will help you to identify the dubious men and to narrow the field to those with whom you're likely to be compatible. Thorough screening is one of the keys to safe and successful online dating.

So, what's the most effective method of screening your prospects? Whether you're responding to a man's emails or text messages or chatting to him on the phone, it's important to ask him about the things that are most important to you and to take careful note of his answers. But clearly there's no substitute for meeting him in person. On a date, you can not only ask more questions, you can also observe how he behaves. In short, you need to be constantly on the lookout for signs that a man is not looking for the same thing you are or that you and he are not compatible for other reasons. Types of behaviour, personal qualities and situations that you probably (and in some cases definitely) shouldn't ignore include the following:

- ▶ The only photo he has posted is a close-up of his face.
  Is he deliberately hiding his whole body? Maybe the photo is many years old? Perhaps he thinks that one pic is enough to convince you he's a catch? Or maybe he just can't be bothered posting more than one photo because he's not seriously looking for a long-term relationship.

- ▶ His first message to you simply says 'Hey'. This tends to suggest that he takes a scattergun approach and contacts all women whose photos he likes in the same way. It's highly likely that he hasn't bothered to read your profile and to find out what sort of person you are or what kind of relationship you are seeking.

- His values are starkly different from yours.
- He isn't curious to find out more about you.
- He says things that are inconsistent with what he's told you previously. This is often a worrying sign.
- He asks you to send him money or to provide him with your banking or credit card details before you've met in person. This would be an alarming development, a massive red flag, and you should never – under any circumstances – agree to do this. Don't be taken in by anything he says or by the depth of your feelings for him. Fraud is very common in online dating, and such a man is almost certainly a scammer. If this situation arises, you should immediately stop contacting him, block him from being able to contact you, report the matter to the dating app, and contact the police.

  And if a man you've met only a few times behaves in this way you need to consider the likelihood that he too is a scammer and that he set out to flatter you and soften you up before trying to get money out of you. In either case, if it turns out that the man concerned is not a scammer but is simply in such dire financial straits that he has asked a virtual stranger, or someone he has known for only a short time, to loan or give him money, he is unlikely to be the one for you.
- You discover that his divorce hasn't been finalised and he's still embroiled in a dispute with his ex-wife about outstanding legal issues. A man in this position is usually in no state to pursue a relationship.
- He 'disappears off the radar' for extended periods of time.
- You receive a text message from him that appears to have been intended for someone else.
- He becomes angry if you don't respond to his text messages or emails immediately.

- He talks too much about his ex or exes. If he describes them all as 'crazy', this should concern you even more.
- He's overly critical and judgmental.
- He asks you to send him explicit photos of yourself before your first date (or, worse still, he sends unsolicited and inappropriate photos to you).
- On your first date he spends a lot of time on his phone (or does this habitually).
- He's frequently and inexcusably late when meeting with you.
- He flirts with female staff at restaurants or treats them poorly.
- He wants to rush into a serious relationship.

Have realistic expectations

Once a man has ticked all your preliminary boxes and you've decided you would like to meet him in person, set up a date as soon as possible. If you're getting on well via text messages and phone calls and this continues for too long, you may develop a 'cyber-crush' on him and build up unrealistic expectations – that's human nature, but it's risky. Putting him on a pedestal is likely to make you especially nervous when you finally meet, and this may make you appear less confident than you usually are or hinder you from just being yourself. Worse still, it can cause a lot of disappointment if things don't work out as you'd hoped. So, meet quickly. Keep your expectations low. And just aim to have a pleasant time.

Keep your first date casual

First dates can be nerve-racking because many people (both men and women) fall into the trap of thinking that every person they meet could be 'the one'. Remember, just because you hit it off during text messages and phone calls, this doesn't mean you'll get on well in person or that you're compatible for a long-term relationship. Placing too much emphasis on the importance of the first date can make your internet dating experiences much more stressful than necessary. So, while it's natural to be cautiously optimistic when meeting men with whom you seem to have good chemistry, try to think about your first dates as being all about socialising and meeting new people. Just relax, be yourself and enjoy your new-found freedom.

Here are some of the unwritten rules for a first date:

- Your personal safety is paramount, so the location of your first date should be somewhere neutral, public and busy, preferably in an area you're familiar with. Never meet a man at his home, and don't allow him to pick you up from yours. If you have a car, it's a good idea for you to drive yourself to the date rather than taking public transport or using a ride-share operator. This will avoid any awkwardness at the end of the date if he offers to take you home.

- Tell a good friend when and where you're meeting your date, and give her his phone number. If it will help to ease your nerves, ask her to call or text you during the date to check that you're OK. If appropriate, call her when you get home so that she knows you're safe.

- Don't meet for a meal. If things aren't going well, it's much easier to excuse yourself and make a quick exit from a casual meeting than it is from a lunch or a dinner.

- Night dates are the norm, but a daytime date tends to have a more casual feel to it and may help you to feel more relaxed. If you want to try something different from the traditional coffee shop or bar rendezvous, go for a stroll along a river or through a popular park. This is conducive to a relaxed atmosphere and, since there's always something to look at, provides plenty of conversation starters to help avoid any awkward moments of silence.

- First impressions count, so dress with care but appropriately for the occasion.
- Smile readily and generally be open and friendly.
- Although it may be tempting to break the ice by sharing details of prior online dating experiences, don't spend much time, if any, on this. After all, the purpose of the date is to get to know one another.
- Don't leave your drink unattended at any time.
- There's no hard and fast rule about who should pay the bill. Just go with whatever feels appropriate.
- Trust your intuition. If it feels all wrong, it probably is.

Dating again after a divorce can be an adventure. You'll have good experiences and bad. But don't be discouraged; this new way of meeting people will take time to master. Dates will not always go as well as you may have expected. Most women, like most men, have a mixed bag of experiences. Online dating is a numbers game, so it's a good idea to keep an open mind and be willing to explore all genuine possibilities. And remember that just because there's no 'lightning bolt' chemistry on the first date, this doesn't necessarily mean you're not a good match. Unless a man is obviously not the one for you, give the relationship a chance – it takes time to get to know someone and also for affection to develop. To quote the first line, which is also the title, of a very fine poem by American poet Robert Creeley, sometimes 'love comes quietly'.

★ ★ ★

www.ingramcontent.com/pod-product-compliance
Lightning Source LLC
Chambersburg PA
CBHW072338300426
44109CB00042B/1722